Say That

MARY BURRITT CHRISTIANSEN POETRY SERIES
Hilda Raz, Series Editor

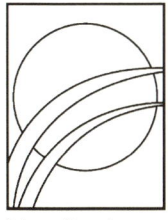

Mary Burritt
Christiansen
Poetry Series

SAY
THAT

Felecia Caton Garcia

UNIVERSITY OF NEW MEXICO PRESS

ALBUQUERQUE

Library of Congress Cataloging-in-Publication Data

Caton Garcia, Felecia Rose, 1974–

 Say that / Felecia Caton Garcia.

    pages cm. — (Mary Burritt Christiansen Poetry Series)

    Poems.

 ISBN 978-0-8263-5316-0 (paper : alk. paper) — ISBN 978-0-8263-5317-7 (electronic)

 I. Title.

 PS3607.A7215S29 2013

 811'.6—dc23

                    2012042767

Composed in Dante MT Std 11.5/13.5

Display type is Dante MT Std

*Dedicated to the memory of
George Albert Garcia and Irma Belle Caton who
dedicated themselves to the mystery of living.
And to my mother, with love.*

Sólo el misterio nos hace vivir. Sólo el misterio.

—FEDERICO GARCÍA LORCA

Contents

Entomology

It begins like a poem: dusk and memory, frogs
  and wheat, cicadas on the sycamore.

Wine blooms fragrant and thick on my tongue.
  The turgid surface of the glass ripples

with the memory of a child: the screen house
  in the corner of the yard and the shivering

nest of spiders, black and long-limbed. Wine
  spills, each drop a dark spider

growing long, irregular legs. *Read them for me*
  you say, as if they were tea leaves

or ideograms. Let's drink to drinking, to memory.
  Let's drink to our fathers who drank

to anything. The fields seethe with insects:
  crickets, mosquitoes, deerflies, bees.

I crouched at my father's feet, *Tell me again*
  about the bees. I know the memories

of our fathers are no more reliable than our own.
  Bees dance in their sweet cells, wasps

build homes in the same rafters, year after year.
  We are watched by memory.

The nests of wasps are made of paper.
  The bottle is empty.

I.

Mirrors

East L.A. in Three Stages of Time

In the morning I paint murals at Chuy's Taquería.
Chuy gives me free tacos and buys my paint,
doesn't mind that I paint and repaint the same wall:

pyramids become Mexican women in blue shawls
become jungles become saints. In the afternoon
I score my chiva and sit on the corner watching

Los Vatos Locos riding toward the American Dream
in clean gaudy cars that won't start. My brother
died three days ago: Sarge, laid out in his coffin

covered in roses and banners reading *Tus Carnales*.
In the hospital bed, he held out his arm and asked
for it: the last dose. I gave it to him. I watched

a young girl carry a baby across the parking lot.

Carnalito, he said, *time slows! And you can almost see it!*

Holy Week Triptych: Mother and Child, Mexico, 1978

Easter Sunday: Oaxaca

The risen Christ moves through the market, trailing
the scent of blood and a pack of dogs. Baskets overflow
with lilies, brim thick with glittering fish. If we were home,

I would feed my daughter the firm flesh of boiled eggs.
Her straw basket would fill with dyed eggs: vermillion,
saffron, azure. Here, we make do with the shells

blown dry. I carried the empty eggs hundreds of miles
south in a sturdy cardboard box. Touching them now,
I taste the viscous yolks I sucked onto my tongue.

We paint them with images of home: chestnut horses,
twisted cottonwoods, black earth, fat red chickens.
My daughter delights in their fragility. She forgets

what's missing. The wonder is not in the flown god,
but in the stone rolled away, the empty and echoing tomb.

Holy Saturday: Tuxtepec

It is hot and the whole town is waiting. All morning we rode
a crowded bus away from the ocean only to sit in the dust

to wait for another. My daughter pulls her small hands
through her hair and twists her damp braids around her head

like a crown. *What are we waiting for?* she asks, restless
in her father's arms. She studies her bare feet, drinks

a bottle of orange Fanta, blows low notes over the top
of the glass. She counts the hollow shells she carries

in her pockets, licks them to make them shine as they did
when she found them in the froth. She sorts and catalogues

the small clattering stacks of empty homes, their soft
inhabitants long since swallowed whole by birds or fish.

I want to go back to the ocean, she tells us, *I want
a sand dollar, some coral.* We tell her it's impossible

to return, and pull from our packs a distraction, a rare
and familiar thing: a sugar egg, a cave of white crystal

decorated with violets and daffodils. Stripes of yellow
and green disguise the seams, hide the unraveling

mystery of the true wonder: in one end of the egg,
a hole wide enough for a child's eye; inside, a diorama

of sugar figurines: a family of ducks, a field of flowers.
An idyllic spring morning in minutiae is enough to enchant

her for an hour, long enough for the bus to arrive.
Days later, when a storm catches us outside of Guadalajara,

melting the delicate construction, her face will register relief,
the burden of keeping this impossible world whole lifted

by the veil of rain.

Good Friday: Veracruz

In the stone chapel overlooking the ocean
        the saints are dressed in mourning,
sleeping, perhaps, under their veils. The priest

seems truly shaken, bearing again the violent
         end, the broken man, uncertain
of the miracle this year. The ocean denies it all,

resplendent in its sequined robes,
         one vast swirl of sunlight on water.
The fishermen begin to sing, think better of it,

and haul their nets in silence. My daughter,
         still for once, stands beside her father
to select three fish

and we begin to slit the taut bellies, to open
         the jeweled packages, to make them
caves of flesh. My child is encrusted with scales,

up to her elbows in blood and shimmer. We cut
         open the swollen belly of the third fish,
and eggs cluster in the wound like gold.

My husband hollows the cavity in one motion,
         cups the mound of watery life
in his palm and displays it. Our daughter takes

the eggs in her hand, each one glistening
         against her skin, cold against the heat
and tremor of her unyielding desire: dying

in spite of her. And I could not save them.
         I could not save any of us.

Tezcatlipoca's Mirror

I watch my father trim his beard with the silver
sewing scissors shaped like a heron. Its beak devours
his soft, dark hair. He meets my eyes in the mirror,

says, *Did you know that Tezcatlipoca sees
everything in his obsidian mirror?*

Everything like what?

Everything.

I am a literal child, but not without imagination.
I ask my father, *How big is his mirror?*

The same size as his eye.

I think about this while my father looks away
from me and tilts his head toward the light.

He is already dying, but we don't know.
The mirror ripples, and I narrow my eyes,
but there is only my father's dark skin, his hands

steady against his own throat. He asks,
Do you believe me about the mirror?

Dreams My Father Told Me

In Which the Mayor Welcomes Him to Town

I'm sitting in Zacatecas eating tortillas, piles of them. A fat Mexican girl cooks them for me and calls me *mitote*, meaningless uproar. After a while, the mayor of the village comes to talk to me. There are thirsty dogs everywhere. I feel things I hadn't felt since I met your mother.

In Which He Remembers His Brother

I'm chasing off the kids from the block who have come to see what's happening. Sarge is lying on the small square of grass in front of the house and I know he's tried to kill himself. The paramedic arrives, a woman, and she cuts off his t-shirt. Around his heart is a wreath of roses. She looks up at me and says, *I remember him now.*

In Which He Is Invited to Play Guitar with Mississippi John Hurt

After a while my hands get tired, so I say to him, like we're old friends, *Hey, John, I've got to rest my hands, man.* And he opens his mouth to answer except the Mississippi River starts pouring out of it, on and on until nearly everything is under water. I'm floating on my guitar in the middle of a thick, dark river. It's like that for a long time.

In Which He Dreams of His Own Death

I'm riding on a bus with Sarge, my mom, and Rose. Shit. What else is there to tell you?

Drought

Try to remember: things go wrong in spite of it all.
I listen to our daughters singing in the crackling
stalks of corn and wonder why I don't love them more.

They move like dark birds, small mouths open to the sky
and hungry. All afternoon I listen to the highway
and watch clouds push down over the hills. I remember

your legs, heavy with sleep, lying across mine. I remember
when the world was transparent, trembling, all shattering
light. I had to grit my teeth against its brilliance. It was nothing

like this stillness that makes it difficult to lift my eyes.
When I finally do, I see you carrying the girls over
the sharp stones of the creek bed. When they pull

at my clothes and lean against my arms,
I don't know what to do and do nothing.

WHIRLAWAY
April 1974

I.
We promenade and allemande. We Box-the-Gnat
        and Shoot-the-Star. We butterfly whirl
and courtesy turn in the church basement

or the Janson's barn. We Swat-the-Flea
        and roll away with a half sashay.
Each woman wears a silver bracelet, each man

a buckle engraved WHIRLAWAY.
        From farms and fields and children
and horses, we've come to step round

and round and catch our partners by the hand.
        We've come to hear the caller,
the fall of the fiddle, the clap of foot on wood.

We Cross-the-Stitch and Do-Si-Do. We best
        the Country Stars and Western Hearts
in our boots and skirts and Sunday best.

II.
I am forty-eight and married to a man whose love
has made him angry. But when we dance, he smiles

at me, isn't worried by my hand on another man's arm,
is willing to be a stranger's hesitant friend. This is what

marriage has come to mean. When the woman
from the kitchen turns to yell over the music, *A call,*

my husband turns, still smiling, to walk away,
and I think: *Remember this.*

III.
We take the corners so fast, I think we will hit the base
of a hickory or sugar maple. My bracelet glitters and rattles
around my wrist in the lights of passing cars. There were two
voices on the phone, the first one, receding, saying, *I can't
do this. I know them. I can't.* And the second voice of a stranger
who says, *There's been an accident. Your son. A curve. A tree.
His body.* I finger the silver letters that dangle from my arm
as if they really were charms, spells, a defense or a faith. I look
at my husband in profile beside me. I think of the rest
of my children waiting at home, the youngest, only twelve,
nothing but freckles and teeth. And, for a moment, I hate them.
I hate them for what comes next: gathering the bits of myself,
looking at my reflection in the rain-stamped window, clenching
my fingers around the sharp edges of the *W*, the *H*, the *I*,
until they bruise. To think I will have to live through this.

Firecracker in a Coke Bottle

My death was spelled out in the constellation
of cigarette ash and ignitions. Flickering, uncertain

combustions in the nights of river-bottom winter.
Even I, nearly blinded by the tight web of the future,

saw something of it in the loose spiral of smoke
from my mouth, in the rafters of the barn

where the moths gathered before dusk.
Long ago, I'd lost my finger to a firecracker

in a Coke bottle. There, in the blood slick
shard of glass, was a doorway, glittering.

Since then, I'd been careful of doors. But there it was,
my last breath, nestled in the wet leaves, bundled

in the needles of the tree, tucked in the tread
of the tires. I'd seen it once before in the brilliant

shatter of the bottle, a forgotten word,
death like *love* or *now*.

Yesterday Mark

I am twelve, but now I am older. I was fifth,
      but now I am fourth. My brother is dead
      but the doctor told us not to tell my sister:

It's too late. She might lose the baby. My sister
      is going to have a baby. So my mother
      washed the pills the doctor gave her down

the sink. She changed her dirty clothes. She washed
      her beautiful red hair. I brushed it dry
      in the yard and she cried. Then she pulled

me into her lap and said, *I am going to see
      your sister. If you come with me, you
      must be able to say his name. You*

must be able to say Mark. You must not cry.
      She held me and said, *You don't
      have to go.* But my sister is having a baby.

I am twelve, but now I am older. I was fifth,
      but now I am fourth. I am going to be
      an aunt and someday I will grow older

than my brother. So I lay my head against my sister's
      belly. I smile and say, *Yesterday, Mark
      took me to the river to play.*

Refrain

Once there was a window: a pan full
of mussels, the blue turning ever more

blue in the heat, a man standing with
his back bent and his face lit with love.

I can't bring this moment back.
Even now it is hidden from me:

his secret, my desire. Our secrets
were always the best of us.

Anaphylaxis

August, and I was mired in the burn of summer. Desire was honey-combed deceit. Lies: I carried them in my pocket and fondled them like stones. This one for luck, this one for lust, this one for an empty stretch of road. We stretched out beneath a honey locust in some farmer's field, bits of stone and bark beneath my back. The hive was nestled in a fork of branches. In memory, the sting is inevitable. (Ask yourself, in hindsight was that lie you told a good idea? Now, without hindsight, ask again.) Bees, after all, are distilled devotion: small, hot bodies of sacrifice. He pulled away from me and watched me save myself: the second sting of the steel syringe to send epinephrine humming through my veins, adrenaline battering the heart like coded wingbeats. We kept the dead bee. Set it on the dash as we drove. We laughed at my near escape, but the welt on my throat was a persistent rune: a swollen caution against abandoning the hive, against trust in the body, against the solitary desire.

Midwest Ranchera

Thursdays, the devil danced at the Black Saddle, cloven
hooves tracking dust for later evidence. He drove a black

Mercury with suicide doors and flames flickering the fins.
Sometimes he slid from the door with his tail forking long

and taut to the floor. Hot-tongued, he would say, *Do you
want to touch it?* And who didn't want to touch that tail?

Black-feathered, hypnotic, a winged serpent moving in time
to the accordion. He would quote from the Bible, his face

crackling with love or fever, luminescent in the Kansas night.
He would slip his arms around hips, hook the tail over

a bare shoulder, and we all knew then there were things more
important than salvation. In his arms, the plain girls became

beautiful. Every man wants to win a woman from the devil.
Her eyes were embers when she followed him out the door,

leaving us glittering and restless with envy, cicadas singing in the heat.

Night Sweats

With you on my back, I fought my way across the field,
the rutted paths of cattle snatching at my feet. Your fingers
laced my throat and your breath cooled against my neck.

The memory of sisters is twinned: we'll each find what we want
in the dusk and drone of regret. But don't tell me the day
didn't wear on. There are things that won't be mistaken for prayer:

the thick fear at the top of the stairs, the shared night sweats
of sisters. You say I don't remember what it was: the festering
swelter of skin and sheet, the incessant aria of the lake:

frog, crickets, fish, snakes, all scale and skin, rustle and ripple.
I carried you through it. I didn't want to, but I did.

Sarah in the Nave

She loved me when lies were my currency, my way
in the world. She sent a postcard of a Mexican devil,

his highball glinting in silver foil: a final clue. But I never
believed in her whetstone, her wheel and her forge. I never

believed in her fury. That was my mistake.
Now I want to lean into her heart and feel that angry hive

thrum against my lips. Where have you been while the winged
things became paper and dust? In the silent speeded film,

wasps build the many-chambered halls of siblings.
I might have been her sister, if I had kept her secrets

closer to my own. But she never had a sister, and I said so.
Forgive me, sister, secret keeper, winged sting.

Territorial Jockeying

Because I love you, the sky is a moving picture, a silent
film where the heroine delivers cloud-drenched soliloquies
before disappearing behind a veil of rain. Because I love
you, I draw a line of salt in the dust. I recite the ritual
farewells of a thousand tongues before scuffing the salt
into the ground: sterile earth until I see you again. Because
I fell in love when the world no longer believes in heroic
death, the Valkyries are replaced with ten thousand
sugar gliders performing *Attack of the Vuvuzelas* while
sweeping out of the sky. Love was always absurd and abused.

Because I love you, I remember his voice saying, *She's asleep.*
She'll never remember. But she did. Because I love you,
the sky, the salt, and the song have all tied themselves
into a unicursal hexagram, an interdimensional knot.
Because I love you, I have given up on the idea of love.

Four Gifts

—*for C. M.*

My flesh was mulched with absence and pain.
The seeds unfurled under my skin: a disordered
scrabble of fruit and flower. And I nurtured

this tangle of growth, do you understand?
This is what I had to make a life. *He who loves*
his child chastises her was the first commandment

in my father's book of days. My spine became
a trellis of thorns, the names of roses became
a litany of endurance: *Bourbon, Belle Story, Peace.*

Children, my father said, *will try to convince you*
they are innocent, defenseless, unsuspecting.
I unearthed sharp rocks, picked berries with bare hands.

The pain, he said, *is in your mind.* Years later,
paralysis a slowly opening violet in the small
of my back, I run ten miles on broken bone.

I didn't feel anything, I tell the doctors again
and again, *I didn't feel anything at all.* Rage
is the wild plum beating at my eyes, the mayapple

knocking at my shins. The broken bark of black locust
and the green hulls of walnuts made the path I walked
until you arrived. I didn't invite you. I never imagined

you might fight your way through the vines of wild grape,
the greasy leaves of poison sumac, tempting toxins
of rosary pea and jessamine. Daughter, unlikely fruit

of this womb, how will I hold you with these overgrown
arms? How will you suck the sour milk of my body? This
is the fourth and final gift: the child and her need,
the mother love coiled deep.

II.

Maps

Animal Nightmare

"If you suffer from lurking or chasing animal dreams,
keep Saint Margaret in mind."

—Judika Illes

1. Flames like salamanders climb her legs; the sun is a hateful bird. He will make this woman burn for him one way or another. I place her on my windowsill, tilt her face toward the light so she will remember.

2. The porcelain cauldron at her feet is chipped; the accessories of secondhand saints are not exempt from ruin. I run my wet finger around the rim. Was it love? *Drop her in*, he said. But she stands again: whole.

3. Third time's the charm. Her head drops to the ground and there's no going back. Does that dirt-filled ear hear my petition against the scratch of claw on wood? How will this woman save me from the ragged panting in the corner? The scales rasping down the tree?

4. I keep her in mind. If this cracked saint drags the hot-furred animals into the light, will I know what to do with them? The fire, the water, the teeth make a strange beast.

Lost Children

I step into their room, pull the blankets
from the bed, and my daughters are gone.
I can't remember the last time I saw them.
I am not surprised. I am desperate with fear.

Don't worry. This is the worst nightmare
of all. It will ride you until you die. Place
a glass of water by your bed. You may
fill it with turpentine, but be warned
that turpentine is falling out of favor,
even with artists. Do not wake in your panic
and drink it. Place two stones in the water
and give them your children's names.

You will not dream this dream again.
Instead, you will be looking for two stones
in a river of stones. Good luck.

Dreams of the Dead (Invitation Declined)

In the dream he says, *Take my hand.*
Take my tongue in your mouth.

My sister tells me this is an inappropriate
request coming from the dead. But how

do you decline an invitation from one
who has already lost so much?

I try the time-tested tactics of women:
evasion, deception. My sister is firm.

She insists there is no room for hesitation,
no empty plate at the table. *Take off*

your shoes and lie on his grave. Tell him
I live in this world and no other.

Put on your shoes. Don't look back.

Hex

From a book I've learned how to send
nightmares like love letters returned to sender.
I'll need red paper, a black goat, coriander,
and blood. Still, the instructions are vague.

They don't say where nightmares breed.
They don't say if they will be like the ones
you had when you slept beside me: my cat,
tiger-sized, pulling you from the bed by your foot.

Or if they will be the nightmares where the hand
reaches to the windowsill to place an apple,
again and again, and all the while you know
something horrible has begun.

Halloween

Tonight all of my nightmares come to the door
decked in black feathers and thick-stitched eyes.

For once the small are powerful, disguised,
demanding, and at our doors. Every bit of this

reminds me of you: old magic tricked out
in synthetic disguise; formulas for extortion:

trick or treat. So I wait for you to call
or to open my gate with your red wings brushing

the hedge full of wasps, your oversized hands reaching
for me through the screen. I haven't forgotten what it is

to be with you, the trick and the treat bundled together
like honey in the hive—a child's voice from under

the sheet. The children make safe passage with screams
of laughter, sequins and foil knives, dark fur and silk

glittering under the streetlights. Impossible not
to remember you and the home you made a cabaret

of fear with my hair in your fists, your voice in my ear:

Trick? Treat? Is it sweet? Will it hurt?
Will you want it anyway?

Refraction

You're cold as St. Elmo's fire or a Children's Book of Verse.
Sun dog, mirage, morgana, the horizon of desire conspires

to render you vivid only at the edge of vision. The shards
buried in you that I mistook for stars? Asterism. Flaws.

You touch me with the strike of the basket's cobra:
heat floods the blood—and then it doesn't. No poison

in the wound, no fever, just a momentary rattle of heart.
You're a parlor trick, a swamp candle, a Mobius loop of want.

Though no one can explain the radical proximity of the moon
at dusk. No earthly curve or atmospheric warp accounts

for the gravid sphere, the brilliance. Distance is in the eye
of the beholder. Only our pointless longing calls it close.

Which begs the question: if there is less to you than meets
the eye, is it you? Or is it my eye? And don't I love

the magic trick? The two-way mirror? The icy flame?
Don't I love what I hear when I lean close to you?

The sound of all that rushing life when you smile at me,
precious and empty as a shell.

Old Love as a Function of Atomic Decay

I rendered my child's mind for you.
Bees, hay, blood-edged blades of grass,
hooves heavy with mud, poison sumac
along the fence, the last hour with my father.

You gave me almost nothing in return.
You gave me depletion. You gave me
the overdrawn account, the tally marks
of the hostage. You stroked my thighs
and crooned about decay the perfect clock
eating up from the ground.

                    I heard it too:
the ticking of atoms, the death of stars, the river
cutting stone. Almost nothing. I took it for granted.

The Queen

You could have been another woman on her knees
in front of a bucket of water, a brush, a woodsman
or a wanderer. Instead, the old crone tapped you

with her stick: a rush of light and you were more than bone,
you were divine. The rise to power is a run of luck: a pair
of kings, a straight flush, snake eyes tattooed on your back.

But the death of a queen is always the crush of her memory.
One day becomes a rout of years; where are your shoes,
your jewels, the mirror that made you blush with its old lie?

Fools!, you cry at the servingmen, *The princess is false!*
Take her into the forest. Crush her pretty neck against the stone.
Queens cannot afford their daughters; the magic is undone.

The trick to keeping the kingdom whole unravels you.

Remains

You kiss ghosts and then they think they own you.
That's my story: ghost kissed and twice lonely.
They'll promise you anything, the dead: eternity,

unwavering devotion, new clothes, the endless swelter
of unfulfilled desire. But all they do is rhyme
and riddle, submit petitions against the dangers

of the flesh. All I did was press my thigh against his,
feed him bread from my hands on a crowded bus.
I wanted and I wanted and then he was dead: bone

and ash and I was alone. I can't help it. I want love
to be like this all of the time. Doesn't everyone?
Some nights he takes my hand, says

I think you'd better come with me.

The Professional Mourner

I.
In spite of myself, I live
in the house on the hill
where I cover the mirrors
and whisper the names
of the dead to bees.
This keeps the honey
dark and sweet. The roof

is planted with lilies
and the rain is the faintest
seep of discontent. Every hour
I set the clocks back forty-two
minutes. In this way I stave
off the chimes and bells
of the dead.

II.
Listen: the silence of the clocks.
It works: the seep, the hum
of bees. Worry leaves this house

alone. I sleep alone in the house
on the hill. I blacken my feet
and face with burnt floorboards

from the study. I study
the profession of mourning.

The Professional Mourner's Competition

The woman in the house on the hill
calls herself a professional mourner.
She's just a poet with a job.

I'm the one down here drowning kittens
and shooting dogs. You have to
inoculate yourself with grief.

When I get to a crossroads, I can't
hesitate. I know which road to take.
When the dirt falls on the coffin

and it starts to rain and everyone,
I mean everyone, mothers, fathers,
wives, children, are running

from the grave with black umbrellas
and yesterday's newspapers over
their heads, I'm the one who stays.

I'm the one who stays to hear
if the dead have anything left to say.
I'm the one who sets the clocks

forward and rings the bells all night.
I don't cover my mirror and I don't
like what I see. Who would?

Who wants to be the last to leave?
Let her bury her bees and burn her house.
This is what I get paid for.

Still Birth

I wish I could open
more easily to light,

to the sound
of my mother

calling for me.
Stillbirth, this

door like no
other, to emerge

silent, closed, drowned
from the safest place.

I was coming
to join you. Then

the waters receded
and not even I

could walk them.
I'd nurse away

the memory of me,
tongue protruding

slightly, like a small
desire left behind.

Weaning

The egg is cold. Its speckled curve nestles
against the flat-bottomed nest, built to rest
deep in the grass and weeds, a roadrunner
or a guinea hen. I know so little about birds.

I know that unhatched eggs in winter mean
nothing good. So when my daughter strokes
the shell, asks *Can we keep it? I will sleep
with it under my pillow*, I know she imagines

an unfurling of tiny wings, a bright eye.
I say, *I don't think this egg will hatch.*

        Well, then, she says,
what will happen to the baby?

At this moment, I would like to pretend
that this girl is not my child. Reader,
I would like her to be yours. You point
to the profusion of feathers on the ground.

Mention the cats, who look away.
Insist, in spite of all you've explained
of birth and hatching, that an egg can be
a coffin. And when this child who still

sleeps with lips moving in the memory
of nursing turns to you and asks,
If you die, will I?, you answer.

Looking for You in Puerto Angel

I have taken to pulling the wings
from mosquitoes before laying

their ruined bodies side by side
where they begin their malarial

feeding on one another. Scorpions
scale the walls of my hotel room,

chattering incessantly about tourists
and hurricanes. Their claws snap

the air like castanets. Each night
I join the other guests on the roof

where every eight seconds the light
from the prison illuminates

our unguarded faces. We drink
to the dry season. We eat

the fish whose sweet, white flesh
is lined with green bones.

Retraction

I'm giving up on the dead. I resign
my membership in the society of mourners.
I leave the ghosts to frighten

unwary children in graveyards.
I want the thick clichés of the living:
lilacs and rain, clandestine embraces

in shadow. I renounce the old, the ashy,
the unrequited desire. Imagine how weary
they are of me and my wanton animation

of their corpses. Where's the peace
of the grave for my unlucky loves?

Touch me here. And here. Hurt me

a little if you have to. Remind me
of the way the living also rasp

and tear. Whisper infractions. Say
full, ripe, strong, fleshy! Say *pulse!*
Suggest lemons on the decks of dark

ships. Suggest something bloody
and beating. Take me somewhere
quivering with meat. Muscles, organs,

and petty jealousies are my new feeding
ground. Take me by the hand.

El Mozote, El Salvador, 1992

The afternoon rain rinses the small hand bones
of children. The archaeologists lift stiff brushes

and carve the earth. Skeletal fingers clutch
a small orange plastic horse. Stiff brushes

clenched in their hands, they sift the red dust.
They whisper the names of the bones: *tibia, metatarsal,*

vertebrae. I want to send death begging on a train,
far from here and hungry. How far could death

get on an orange plastic horse? All around me
is the song of common words: mirror, comb, child's shoe.

We are here to discover what happened then,
but I want to know what happens now.

The gray sky is a stroke of luck. My fingers
clutch the small hand bones of children.

The Bank of Hell

Maybe you worry about what you owe the dead,
that all that is left unredeemed in the day
might be called for in the night. You know

they are gambling in the woods, where the fire
is too hot and the knucklebones of babies
are rolled like dice. You remember the abortions:

the little hands you didn't want to hold. You
find you are afraid of ghosts. You think
the bank of hell deals in a currency you hold.

I, also, am afraid. I am afraid this silence
won't be broken by the scratch of match
in an empty room, the smell of my father's

cigarette. I am afraid of the dirt undisturbed,
the stone unturned. What if it was only ever
our own hands moving across the Ouija board?

Our own knees rattling the table? Give me
the bracelet of bones around my ankle,
the cold wind in the hall. Give me the shadow,

the foot on the stair. I am afraid the dead
are bitter as lovers. What if I burn all the candles,
fill the red envelopes with money,

put that graveyard dust under my tongue,
and they still never speak again? What then?

This Is How We Kill 'em in Suicide Country

The slide guitar is a story bound by wire, wound
too tight and tightening to an infinite quaver:
>*darker days than this and you'll set yourself on fire*

Maybe it's better to forget me now that you've outgrown
the cradle that I made you, the shoes I gave you. Better not to know:
>*the train's a hungry line and each flatbed is a bier*

And when the brakes catch on the rusting rails, it's a choir
bound to sing like it was bound with wire. The gamblers
play with guns, and everyone's a liar. There's no air
to set the chamber on fire:
>*no bullet in the gun doesn't mean that it won't fire*

The radio's infected too, no fear. It's tuned to the white
noise of the savior: his head, his ribs, his story bound
by wire. The full moon's like a lake, the crescent's like a dagger,
the musicians and the gamblers never tire:
>*you said the heart's too dangerous to burn but you're a liar.*

Infidel

If I told you I believed
in your skin as men believe

in God, would you grieve
for me as one who leaves

in your skin, or so men believe,
traces of venom? A tidal scar

for me as one who leaves
the windows open, the door ajar?

Traces of venom? A tidal scar
tracing rain on the window?

The windows open, the door ajar,
I found a port, embarked into shadow.

Tracing rain on the window,
I found a darker path, a track.

I found a port, embarked into shadow.
It's too late to unravel this pact.

If I found a darker path, a track
into God, would you grieve?

It's too late to unravel this pact.
Even if I told you I believed.

Say That

each day in Santiago the disappeared left coffee scalding
on the stove, or a phone ringing in the searing light

of afternoon. When the army set fire to the students,
I fled. Blackened ghosts plucked at my heels, singed

the soles of my shoes. Exiled, I envied all but the dead
their shallow homes. When I found you rooted

in my belly, I wanted to refuse you. Say that on the way
to the clinic, I passed a field of sunflowers. Say that

their raised heads of fire roared across the hill. Say
that I stopped the car, went home. Say that when you

crashed through my body in a tangle of pain, I spread
my bones over the dark ember of you.

Say that you burst into being. Into flame.

The Garden Enclosed

—after a painting by David Jones

I.
Everyone wants to pretend it's a doll
though it is clearly a child lying dead

on the path below. The wooden swing
is abandoned and possibly she fell,

frightened by the harsh sound of geese
tearing through the forest. Twisted

and arched, it is also possible the trees
threw her at the arc of her swing. Perhaps

only the geese have noticed.

II.
The young woman is frightened, but the artist
is insistent: his hands at her waist, the flowers

he has thrust into her hands. The sideways look
of her eye might mean she knows something

terrible has happened. The gray-green sky means
high wind. His mouth is hot on her face, her cheek

mirrors the sky. How could she have known what
they meant, the old women, saying *to love is to bury.*

The Cartographer Returns from Hell

It isn't what you'd think, he told us finally,
after weeks alone in his cluttered office.

Though my sense of direction was compromised,
there are no rings, no levels. It's all flat as Kansas.

Here the cartographer chuckled at his own
midwestern prejudice. *I've finished it,*

the map. And, from the black leather tube
strapped to his back, he pulled the thing

and unrolled it on the table. *Thin lines mark*
well-traveled paths. Slashed lines are little

more than crushed grass and bracken, and,
he said, finger tracing a scant centimeter

above the paper's surface, *these thick lines*
here are the borders. There was a collective

intake of breath, a turning away from
the cartographer from whom came suddenly

the sharp scent of smoke, the acrid taste
of electrical fire, the ripple of unimaginable loss.

Runes

1.
The desiccated beetle in its verdigris
carapace, horizontal to the broken
fork; quartz studded concrete
facing west: *danger from within.*

2.
Seven petals from the ornamental
plum; five blades of grass intersecting
the stone: *no even numbers for lock
and key.*

3.
Twenty steps from the stairs
to the door; sixteen stripes of light
vertical to the grain of wood:
no penance.

4.
Three doctor's notes, illegible,
one lost paycheck; finally, two
times the need to explain: *I
couldn't step through the door.*

5.
Two blue pills and three green
scattered on the napkin. Three
triangles, the sudden hush
in the street below: *momentum.*

Acknowledgments

I gratefully acknowledge the editors and literary journals in which these poems, sometimes in slightly different versions, first appeared:

- "The Queen," "Weaning," and "Lost Children" appeared in *Prairie Schooner.*
- "Advice for a Daughter" and "East L.A. in Three Stages of Time" appeared in *Blue Mesa Review.*
- "El Mozote, El Salvador, 1992," appeared in *The Indiana Review.*
- "Summertime" and "Drought" appeared in *The Northwest Review.*

Early versions of some of these poems also appeared in the chapbook *¡Pos Órale!*, published in 1998 as part of The Chicano Chapbook Series edited by Gary Soto.